The Russian
Museum

PAINTING

Aurora Art Publishers. Leningrad

Introduced and compiled by N. Novouspensky

Г $\frac{80103\text{--}192}{023(01)\text{--}74}$ без объявления

The Russian Museum of Leningrad is a treasure-house of Russian art which has acquired world-wide fame. All branches of Russian fine arts are exhaustively represented here, and it is in this above all that it differs from all other Soviet museums. Its more than 250,000 items consist of numerous samples of the art and handicrafts of Old Russia, a most imposing collection of painting and sculpture, scores of thousands of drawings, water-colours and engravings and, finally, priceless works of decorative and applied art.

The collection of paintings (approximately 9,000 in number) boasts magnificent canvases by the most prominent Russian artists, reflecting all the most important stages in the history of Russian art from the early eighteenth century to the present day.

It was in March 1898 that the doors of the first State museum of Russian art were thrown open to the public. The collections were put on show in the Mikhailovsky Palace, one of the most illustrious architectural monuments of the Russian Empire style, built in 1819—25 to the design of the architect Rossi, who was also responsible for the interior decoration of the palace. Some forty years ago the adjacent building, put up at the turn of the twentieth century to the design of the architect L. Benois, was assigned to the Museum for use as an exhibition hall. The rooms of the so-called Rossi wings, originally occupied by the palace's maintenance services, were also converted into show-rooms. To this day these buildings house the collections of the Russian Museum, but since then great changes have taken place in their composition and in the exhibition now on display in its 120 halls.

The Museum's collection of paintings numbered in the beginning only 434 pieces. These consisted of works by Russian artists which were transferred from the Museum of the Academy of Arts and the Hermitage, from royal palaces and private collections. The various periods, styles and the most important artists were unevenly represented. The Museum had on display almost all of the better-known paintings of the artists of the Academic school and practically none at all by early eighteenth century masters. Works of art of the second half of the nineteenth century were also few in number, though even then several magnificent canvases created by artists of that period had been acquired. The exposition as a whole was a random assemblage of works not compiled on any scientific principle, which, incidentally, was true of most of the then existing museums.

Nevertheless, the inauguration of the Museum was a significant event in the cultural life of the whole country. The numerous visitors (more than 100,000 in the very first year) were shown the famous Russian masterpieces: Briullov's *The Last Day of Pompeii*, Bruni's *The Bronze Serpent*, Repin's *The Zaporozhye Cossacks Writing a Mocking Letter to the Turkish Sultan*, Surikov's *Yermak's Conquest of Siberia*, portraits by Levitsky, Borovikovsky, Kiprensky, Kramskoy and many other outstanding paintings.

The existence of two such museums as the Tretyakov Gallery in Moscow and the Russian Museum in St. Petersburg with widely differing collections helped specialists to reconstruct the overall picture of the history of Russian art. The writings of I. Grabar and A. Benois, published in the 1900s, laid the groundwork for serious and systematic research on the creative activity of Russian artists of various periods.

After the October Revolution thousands of wonderful works of art entered the Museum from palaces, mansions and estates, and the best creations of Russian artistic genius, hitherto inaccessible to the public at large, were placed on show. New departments were inaugurated, such as those devoted to decorative and applied art, to folk art, and the Department of Soviet artists (now of Soviet art, one of the largest in the Museum) began receiving its first entries. Soon after the October Revolution the display was reorganized on the scientific and historical principles, the aesthetic side being duly taken into account. The Museum was gradually being transformed into a truly scientific institution, a real shrine of art.

The 145 paintings reproduced in this album have been selected for publication because they are the most widely known and the most representative of their period. The album opens with reproductions of canvases executed 250 years ago and rounds up with works by contemporary artists.

The reforms which were effected during the early eighteenth century, the ruthless disruption and the reshaping of feudal Russia, the difficult war against foreign invaders and the tempestuous development of the country were all factors which contributed to the emergence of realistic art in Russia, an art which tore itself loose from the stranglehold of medieval scholastic dogmas and caught up with the European culture that had long before undergone its own "renaissance". Prompted by society's needs, Russian art became infected with the bustling spirit of the times, centering its attention on the active, vigorous personality. This naturally led to the predominance of the portrait. However, the flourishing of the portrait genre is not confined to this period exclusively, but to the eighteenth century as a whole, which produced a large group of remarkable portrait painters.

The first experiments in portrait painting can be observed in the so-called *parsuna* art (portrait icon) of the close of the seventeenth century. A typical case in point is the *Portrait of Yakov Turgenev, the Jester of Peter I.* The powerful and laconic individual characterization combines here with a somewhat conditional, planar brushwork, which points to the unknown artist's affinity with the traditions of icon painting.

Works by artists of a later period also bore to a certain extent the imprint of the icon tradition, for example A. Antropov's *Portrait of M. Rumiantseva.* The twenties of the eighteenth century, however, saw the emergence of a new, realistic manner in portraiture, which testified to the further development of the portrait genre in Russia. Two of the most outstanding exponents of this novel style of the Petrine epoch were Ivan Nikitin and Andrey Matveyev. Both were sent abroad by Peter I to perfect their skill and display their craftsmanship while so doing. Having fully mastered the technique of Western European art, they nevertheless lost none of their own artistic individuality. Features of Russian life are portrayed in the mature works of these masters with power and accuracy and their artistic interpretation of reality is typical of Russian art as a whole.

Nikitin's portraits of Peter I and the Hetman of the Ukraine, though laconic and austere, recreate strictly individual images of these forceful and manly personalities. The paintwork of the canvases is reserved and full of an inner tensity. In the double portrait of A. Matveyev and his wife one senses a warm sincerity beneath the superficial aspects of the epoch — the affected poses and stereotype gestures. Executed in the fifties of the eighteenth century by I. Vishniakov, the childhood portrait of Sarah Fermore has about it a lightsome, poetic aura.

In spite of the fact that the prevailing atmosphere in the royal court and in the salons of the aristocracy (and consequently in works of art) was one of mannerism, the most outstanding Russian painters managed to rise above the glitter of court etiquette and penetrate the inner world of their subjects. This is true above all of the great Russian portraitists

Rokotov, Levitsky and Borovikovsky. The technical perfection of their painting goes hand in hand with its meaningful profundity, with the warm-hearted amiability of the images. Levitsky reproduced with unsurpassed skill the beautiful satins and velvets of his subjects' rich garments, but this is by no means his principal achievement — all his portraits are profound character studies. The lively gaze of the portrayed, the subtle mimicry of their faces reflect unfeigned human feelings. Thus, for example, his Smolny Institute schoolgirls engaged in enacting affected pastoral scenes are the very personification of Youth itself in all its loveliness and charm.

Borovikovsky's portraits represent an attempt to convey the subject's fleeting emotions, to express his pensive, visionary moods and capture the delicate nuances of spiritual uplift. The artist frequently introduced landscapes into his portraits as backdrops, and these played an important role in the character study.

Though the eighteenth century in Russian art was to a great extent the age of the portrait, it saw the emergence of other genres as well. The works of F. Matveyev and S. Shchedrin heralded the birth of landscape painting: the first to appear were scenes of palace parks and other picturesque views. At the turn of the nineteenth century F. Alexeyev broke away from the canons of "scenic" painting and created the first urban, architectural landscapes: he is at his exquisite best in those of his canvases which reflect the beauty and lyric harmony of St. Petersburg. Some time later S. Shchedrin produced his poetic pictures of Italy, alive with its humid air, gentle sea and mountain haze. Gone were the staffage figures of people and animals; the artist depicted in their stead the merry, impetuous animation of the Neapolitan esplanades and languid scenes on shady vine-laced terraces. At times this aura of bustling life in his landscapes would take on a romantic tint.

In the thirties and forties of the nineteenth century the great A. Ivanov, working on his immense canvas *Christ Appearing before the People*, executed numerous preliminary studies, which can be regarded as remarkable independent paintings in their own right, not infrequently unique artistic revelations. Ivanov painted a multitude of open-air nude studies and landscapes proper. This was the first ever attempt in the history of world art to tackle the problem of *plein air* painting.

The genre of history painting made its debut in Russia also in the eighteenth century and by its end had grown to be the dominant form. The decisive factor here was the inauguration in St. Petersburg in 1757 of the Academy of Arts, which for some eighty years remained the only institution in the country turning out professionally trained artists. The Academy became the focal point in the implementation of official policy concerning the fine arts. It stood for an exalted art of great ideological content inculcating patriotism and a sense of civic duty. The genre of history painting seemed to best serve this purpose. The history of every nation can yield many examples of heroic exploits, noble deeds and self-sacrifice on the part of its outstanding personalities. Students of the Academy were encouraged to reproduce these themes in their works. Since the style of classicism was predominant in the Academies the world over, it was equally natural for the St. Petersburg Academy to adhere to it as well.

The doctrine of classicism engendered a number of purely academic conventions in painting: the approach was rationalistic, based on strict rules of draughtsmanship, composition and colour scheme. In their quest for heroic themes the academic artists turned, as a rule, to the events and legends of classical antiquity and above all to those of Ancient Rome because of the highly developed sense of civic awareness of its society. The basic feature of academic art was that it attempted to emulate the classics of the Italian Renaissance. This gave rise to the development of a school from whose ranks many an outstanding master was to emerge, authors of quite a number of socially and artistically significant canvases that are a source of pride to the Russian art of the first half of the nineteenth century.

The merits and the shortcomings of classicism were in full measure evident in the Russian academic school of painting. One must admit, however, that the artists' undeviating interest in national themes was a positive factor. Many of the masters often introduced elements of contemporary problems into the historic legends of their canvases.

The growth of national consciousness, the upsurge of patriotic feelings brought about by the war of 1812 laid their imprint on the historic canvases executed at that time. The progressive elements of society sometimes discerned in these paintings evocations of true patriotism and self-sacrifice for the sake of the people. As a rule, the strengthening of the democratic tendencies in the social consciousness of the people is accompanied by the flourishing of realism in art. This regularity manifested itself in the history of nineteenth century Russian culture, with the realistic trend in painting growing predominant as early as the twenties and thirties, largely outside the walls of the Academy. One of the most notable artists of the nineteenth century was Orest Kiprensky who, while further developing the traditions of the great portraitists of the preceding century, was the first to depict in so unequivocal a manner the nobility of spirit, strength of emotions and perspicuity of thought of his personages. Many of Kiprensky's portraits are imbued with a romantic uplift.

In that same period a new page in the history of Russian art was opened by A. Venetsianov. Making it a rule to reflect nature and the life around him in painstaking detail, he created images of Russian peasants which revealed the human dignity and the intrinsic beauty of the serfs. The unprecedented development of Russian genre painting began with Venetsianov's small-size canvases depicting the common people as their heroes and central figures. His works were the first to portray nature in truthful and poetical images, a nature inseparably linked with the life of the peasant.

As time went on, the fresh breeze of realism penetrated even into the Academy of Arts, forcing its most gifted students to overstep the boundaries of the aesthetic standards imposed on them. This was most vividly reflected in the works of the last grand master of the Academic school, K. Briullov, whose creative career encompasses the period when, in addition to realism, romanticism was becoming the dominant trend in Russian art.

Greatly impressed by what he saw at archaeological excavations near Naples, Briullov produced the gigantic canvas *The Last Day of Pompeii* in which a tragedy of the distant past, the destruction of that city by the eruption of Vesuvius, is reproduced with tremendous force. Striving for historic authenticity, Briullov made the fates, characters, actions and emotions of his subjects the leitmotif of the composition, accentuating preeminently the force and noble dignity of human feelings. The people in Briullov's masterpiece are beautiful, but this is not because he borrowed their likenesses from ancient statues, which was the usual practice among the artists of the academic school. He saw human beauty in the features of the Italians of his day, sketching them from nature. This explains the all-pervading vibrancy

8

and dynamism of the picture, this is why it produces such a powerful impact even on the modern viewer.

The stamp of romanticism is also apparent in the canvases of the Russian seascape painter I. Aivazovsky. The motifs of his paintings were shipwrecks, storms at sea, man's struggle with the majestic and ominous elements and the magic charm of a moonlit sea. His works are distinguished by an emotional intensity and that solemn beauty which is ever present in the sea and which he expressed with such uncanny skill.

By the mid-nineteenth century Russian realistic art had come to a new and very significant turning point. A contemporary of Briullov, the incomparable P. Fedotov manifested profound psychological insight in his small-size but astonishingly cogent canvases devoted to the everyday life of "little" people. In the dramatic, at times even comic situations of his pieces, in his typological characterization, he managed to reveal the intrinsic content of social phenomena just prior to the upsurge of the liberation movement in Russia.

Fedotov's *The Major's Marriage Proposal*, for example, is at first glance only a family scene, interesting and a bit on the funny side. But behind the all too obvious interrelationships of the personages one can descry whole social groups and classes, their typical traits, their historic destinies. The scene is presented in a humorous vein, but the spectator is stirred to active meditation. This applies to every one of Fedotov's thematic canvases, only his smile would sometimes give way to great commiseration for human suffering and to a condemnation of injustice. Fedotov loved people and was highly sensitive to the goodness inherent in their souls, the charm of youth and the strength that lay in kindness. His portrait miniatures express this attitude in a moving and artless way, especially in the charming, natural and maidenly pure image of N. Zhdanovich at the piano. Fedotov was the father of the critical realism which determined the development of Russian art in the second half of the nineteenth century.

The democratic ideals of the time were exceptionally vividly expressed in the œuvre of V. Perov. His painting *A Meal in the Monastery* is a scathing denunciation of church morals. The picture *Solitary Guitar Player*, on the other hand, is full of compassion for the lonely impoverished old man and permeated with a lyrical sadness. From then on man and his spiritual world, his needs, aspirations and sorrows, the social problems of the day — these became the central themes of all honest, progressive-minded artists.

1870 saw the formation of the Society for Circulating Art Exhibitions, and a year later, in December 1871, it held its first exhibition. This was an event of the utmost significance not only in the artistic, but in the social life of Russia as well. The movement of the Itinerants, as they came to be called, became synonymous with all that was progressive in the fine arts of the country. Champions of truth and humanism, the Itinerants were innovators in all genres of painting who saw anew the purport of social phenomena and proclaimed the new meaning of art itself. The centre of attention of this new art became the everyday life of the people, their present and past, the natural environment they lived in.

The ideological leader of the Itinerants in the seventies was Ivan Kramskoy, a painter who worked mainly in the portrait genre and whose artistic heritage includes a whole picture gallery of his contemporaries from all walks of life, from the intelligentsia to the peasantry. Like the other Itinerants Kramskoy would lay bare the spiritual, inner world of the sitter, regarding it as the mainspring of the image. The portrait of the peasant Miná Moiseyev featured in this album contains all the elements of this approach; it is a typical example of Kramskoy's œuvre, rating among the best of his creations.

The Itinerants introduced a new approach to the then widespread religious motif in painting. Thus, in the *Last Supper* by one of the Society's founding members, N. Gay, an original and profound artist, the evangelical legend is presented as a human, psychological and moral drama. The Itinerants and other like-minded artists glorified the simple unfading beauty of the rural scene. The conventional village motif acquired in their canvases both poetic meaning and social colouring through, above all, its clearly expressed ties with the life of the people.

A gentle lyric [i]sm is also felt in the works of F. Vasilyev, a talented artist whose life span was very brief. His *Scene on the Volga. Barques* is a passionate hymn of praise to the radiant enchantment of a summer morning on the Volga.

The majestic power of Russian nature was the subject of the monumental epic canvases of Ivan Shishkin in which a perfect union of motif and composition was achieved thanks to the artist's excellent knowledge of the forest. Among his finest works reproduced in this album are *Oaks* and the *Mast-tree Grove*.

The heritage of Arkhip Kuinji occupies a place apart in Russian art. Vivid sunsets, cold moonlight shimmering on the waters of a river in the steppe, green birches or eternal snows bathing in blinding sunlight — these are his themes. Kuinji tackled the most difficult of problems in painting, the problem of reproducing light effects, by saturating his canvases with colour and emphasizing the principal elements of form and of colour combinations. As a result there is a decorative quality about his pictures which, however, does not impair their faithfulness to nature and serves to enhance their lofty romanticism.

All the finest achievements of the Itinerants in landscape painting were concentrated in the eighties and nineties in the œuvre of Isaak Levitan, a pupil of and successor to Savrasov and Polenov. His was a landscape reflecting a state of mind, a landscape where the image of the countryside is spiritually enriched with human emotions and where these emotions are expressed through the various states of nature. Levitan's manner is simple and extraordinarily subtle and artistic. His last canvas *The Lake. Russia* completed, by and large, the evolution of Russian landscape painting of the second half of the nineteenth century. It is a poem about the Motherland in all its natural beauty and majestic grandeur.

The greatest Russian artists of the second half of the nineteenth century were Ilya Repin and Vasily Surikov. It was in their canvases that the typical features of the art of the Itinerants were most completely expressed. Repin devoted his amazing talent mainly to depicting life in the Russia of his day; Surikov caused a virtual revolution in history painting by making the people the principal motive force of past historical events.

A brilliant painter and draughtsman, Repin left to posterity portraits, historic canvases and genre pictures unsurpassed in the power of their imagery and the depth of their philosophical insight. One of his finest creations is the *Volga Boatmen*. This painting became both an indictment of the social order and a hymn of praise to the noble character of the masses and the moral strength of the Russian peasant.

Repin's portraits constitute a whole gallery of his contemporaries. It was in this genre that his genius manifested itself most vividly. His portrait of V. Stasov, who waged an incessant struggle for realism in art, is one of the artist's best creations. In the portrait of Pobedonostsev, one of the most bitter enemies of freedom in Russia, the killing characterization given him by the artist is achieved by the merest shade of a hint, so vague as to be almost imperceptible; a broad but dwindling brushstroke merges with the indeterminate outlines to capture the pallid features and the cold expression of Pobedonostsev's face.

In Repin's *The Zaporozhye Cossacks Writing a Mocking Letter to the Turkish Sultan* the story of Cossack freedom in the seventeenth century is, as it were, brought to life. Each personage is characterized in a convincing and extremely vivid manner and the whole scene is full of a spontaneous, irrefutable truth. The free, sweeping brushstroke itself is no less expressive of the life-asserting spirit of the composition than the figures of the Cossacks.

In the œuvre of Surikov the national character that developed in the course of history is reflected with penetrating insight. His was an entirely novel approach to history in that he believed it to be the result of actions by the popular masses, actions which he depicted with the clarity and perception of an eyewitness. The spirit of times gone by is resurrected by the artist in the *Taking of a Snow Fortress* wherein both the poetic compositional structure and the brushwork are radiant and full of the joy of living.

The development of Russian art of the second half of the nineteenth century was crowned by the creation of a number of brilliant canvases, living symbols of the golden age of realistic painting the like of which no other country in the world could boast of at the time.

By the close of the 1880s Russian art stood at the threshold of a new stage in its evolution. The complex and contradictory development of the country's art of the late nineteenth — early twentieth centuries was a result of Russia entering into the age of imperialism, whose characteristic features were sharp social contrasts, an ensuing conflict of ideas and hence a confrontation of two cultures. Subjectivistic aesthetic views and the formalistic trends in art that are their outcome were spreading over the country. The intensification of the struggle for liberation which marked the advent of the third or proletarian period of the revolutionary movement and the progressive artistic intelligentsia's deeply embedded realistic traditions were the main factors which helped the most outstanding artists develop and enrich the very concept of realism and create a vivid and original art.

One of the most gifted artists of this period was V. Serov, a pupil of Repin. He was the author of masterpieces in all genres of pictorial art, particularly portrait painting. Whatever theme he took up, he would lay bare its immanent character with acute insight, poetic force and unmatched artistry. The portrait gallery which he created includes every type of image: some are mellow and romantic, others relentlessly sarcastic, but all are based on awareness of life's truth and hinge on its precise portrayal by the artist.

The great M. Vrubel was an artist inclined toward fantasy and romanticism in the loftiest understanding of these words. He carried the viewer away into the world of the fairy tale, folklore and the poetry of Pushkin and Lermontov. The exalted, symbolic images of his pictures are charged with deep philosophic meaning and are full of an inner tension. Vrubel's painting is possessed of a beauty, integrity and expressiveness all its own, his colours sparkle like precious stones, reflecting both the loveliness of the universe and the spiritual generosity of the artist himself.

A. Benois and K. Somov, two of the most illustrious artists of the World of Art, a society which played a major role in the development of twentieth century art, devoted themselves largely to the idyllic portrayal of the way of life and the art of the past. They were particularly fond of the architecture and the landscape gardening of seventeenth century France and eighteenth century Russia, possessing a precise and penetrating eye for their specific charm. At times the elegant pictures of these artists bear a trace of the ironic, and this is especially true of Somov's works. The World of Art member-artists were also very active in book illustration and stage set designing, raising these two fields to a high level of perfection. They also did a great deal to popularize Russian art in Western European countries.

While speaking of the early twentieth century artists whose works are on show in the Russian Museum mention should be made of A. Arkhipov, a follower of the tradition of the Itinerants, A. Golovin, that great master of theatrical decor, Ph. Maliavin, the author of vivid canvases devoted to Russian rural life, N. Roerich, an archaeologist and painter whose works abound in symbolism and fantasy, B. Kustodiyev and K. Yuon, those poets of the Russian provincial scene, V. Borisov-Musatov with his melancholy and gentle dream-like images, and I. Mashkov, the author of the vibrant, glowing still life, so Russian in spirit.

This list is in itself sufficiently indicative of the diversity of Russian art in the pre-revolutionary years which became part of the history of Soviet art.

The October Revolution opened up a new chapter in the evolution of Russian art. The outstanding artists of the preceding period and the large number of artists who emerged with the establishment of the new social system all contributed to the creation of the art of socialist realism, an art varied in form, but one in ideological content. It became an inalienable part of the ideology of Soviet society, a powerful medium in the shaping of their consciousness and a chronicler of the events of the Revolution.

In the very first years after the Revolution works were produced depicting the heroic reality of that period, the new way of life, the changes being effected in the country and the struggle to protect the achievements of the Revolution. Thus, in 1921 Kustodiyev painted a large decorative canvas called *Festivities Marking the Opening of the Second Congress of the Comintern, May 19, 1920* in which by stressing the rhythmic play of colours and employing the technique of theatrical decor he succeeded in re-creating the atmosphere of a revolutionary holiday enlivened by the people's joy of their newly found freedom.

1923 saw the inauguration of the Association of Artists of Revolutionary Russia (AARR), an offshoot of the Itinerants' movement which was to have a great impact on the evolution of socialist realism in art. The Association set itself the task of depicting through the medium of realistic art all the aspects of the everyday life of the Soviet people after the Revolution. A typical painting of this AARR period is Ye. Cheptsov's *Marking Cooperative Day in a Village*, which is reproduced in this album.

Artists representing other trends who had won recognition in pre-revolutionary times were also successfully coping with Soviet themes. Of particular interest in this respect was the work of K. Petrov-Vodkin.

In the thirties the ranks of Soviet artists were reinforced by a number of young masters who had received their training at Soviet art schools. By this time the Soviet people had launched on the building of Socialism and life was posing new problems before art. In 1932 the Union of Soviet Artists was formed, uniting under its auspices the best masters of various artistic groups. A sizeable portion of the works of most Soviet artists was devoted to the historico-revolutionary theme. Frequently artists who were active in other genres would take it up as well. A case in point is the landscapist A. Rylov, who in 1934 created an interesting canvas entitled *Lenin in Razliv*, a composition imbued with a romantic uplift, where the landscape is by no means a mere backdrop, but a most important medium of emotional expression.

Portraiture is an art wholly devoted to human beings. It is only natural, therefore, that the most significant works to reveal the character of Soviet men and women appeared in precisely this genre. Common to all the portraits was the accent placed on the active, creative nature of Soviet men and women. In this connection a typical example is the portrait of the surgeon S. Yudin by M. Nesterov, one of the oldest of Soviet artists. The transformation which the work of this outstanding master underwent during his Soviet years is symbolic. In it is reflected the overall evolution of Russian art after the October Revolution. In pre-revolutionary times Nesterov had won renown for his lyrical treatment of religious motifs; after the Revolution he attained remarkable success as a portrait painter whose images were always realistic, comprehensive and life-asserting.

The ordeals which the Soviet Union underwent during the War of 1941—45 did not arrest the development of art. The artists' ties with the people became closer still. The events which so shook the nation gave birth to powerful paintings imbued with patriotism and emotional force. One of the most remarkable paintings of that period is A. Deyneka's *The Defence of Sevastopol*. In the fight to the death between Black Sea sailors and the Hitlerites the artist symbolized the irreconcilable, passionate resistance of the entire Soviet people to the Nazi onslaught. The ideological content of the canvas is conveyed through the utmost emotional tension of the composition in a laconic painterly style.

A. Plastov's depiction of man's daily life is coloured by a poetic appreciation of nature. The main motif of his canvases is the new life of the collective farmer. Rich, lush colours and bold brushstrokes characterize Plastov's *Midday*, *Summertime* and *Vitia the Herdsboy*.

The plates featured on the last pages of this album are illustrative of the creative endeavour of the Soviet artists of the recent period and testify to their achievements. These paintings are currently on show in the Russian Museum. One of the most impressive is the picture *The Reds Have Come* in which the Leningrad artist Yevsey Moiseyenko develops the principal line of his work: the romantic theme devoted to the Civil War.

G. Korzhev's canvas *Parting* is notable for its compositional scheme, its laconicism and sincerity. As far back as the thirties and forties S. Chuikov, a subtly lyrical artist and a colour-wizard, created magnificent poetic images of the people and scenery of Soviet Kirghizia. To this day it is his favourite theme. In the fifties Chuikov painted a series of pictures devoted to India.

The technique of one canvas amalgamating the elements of a genre painting, a portrait and a landscape to form one organic whole was born in the sixties. This renders the composition of the painting profounder and more complex, thus allowing for a deeper penetration into the manifold and interrelated laws of life. Soviet artists strive to bring out the active, dynamic qualities inherent in man; that is why their representations deliberately stress typological features rather than any portrait likeness. Worth mentioning, for instance, are such paintings as *Birthday Party* by O. Bogayevskaya, *Polar Explorers* by the Smolin brothers, *On a Warm Day* by A. Levitin, *Mothers' Thoughts* by A. Yeriomin. Though executed in different painterly techniques, these canvases reveal the definitive aspects of the Soviet people of today, and as such are illustrative of the Soviet way of life. The utmost generalization is thereby achieved without, however, blurring the essential characteristics of the image.

The canvases by Soviet artists reproduced in this album will serve to acquaint the reader with the typical features and historical background of Soviet art and with the individual pictorial language of the most outstanding of its representatives.

The vast number of exhibits in the Russian Museum's collection, and the constant research that is carried out on them, facilitates the working out of a new apprehension of the heritage of the past and covers all the trends in contemporary art.

The number of visitors to the Russian Museum is constantly growing. The Museum's work with the public helps to give ordinary people a true appreciation of the treasures they have inherited, treasures which are now in their sacred charge.

Plates

1

Unknown painter. First quarter of the 18th century
Portrait of Yakov Turgenev, the Jester of Peter I
Oil on canvas. 105 × 97.5 cm

ꙖКОВЪ : ТУРꙀГЕНЕВЪ :

2

Ivan Nikitin. *C.* 1688—1741
Portrait of the Hetman of the Ukraine. 1720s
Oil on canvas. 76 × 60 cm

3

Ivan Nikitin. *C.* 1688—1741
Portrait of Peter I. First half of the 1720s
Oil on canvas. 55 × 55 cm (circular)

4

Andrey Matveyev. 1701—1739
Self-portrait of the Artist with His Wife. 1729 (?)
Oil on canvas. 75.5 × 90.5 cm

5

Ivan Vishniakov. 1699—1761
Portrait of Sarah-Eleanor Fermore. 1750s
Oil on canvas. 138 × 114.5 cm

6

Alexey Antropov. 1716—1795
Portrait of M. Rumiantseva. 1764
Oil on canvas. 62.5 × 48 cm

7

Alexey Antropov. 1716—1795
Portrait of F. Krasnoshchokov. 1761
Oil on canvas. 56 × 47 cm

8

Ivan Argunov. 1727—1802
Portrait of E. Lobanova-Rostovtseva. 1754
Oil on canvas. 81.5 × 62.5 cm

9

Fiodor Rokotov. 1730s—1808
Portrait of V. Surovtseva. Second half of the 1780s
Oil on canvas. 67.5 × 52 cm (oval)

10

Fiodor Rokotov. 1730s—1808
Portrait of I. Orlov. Between 1762 and 1765
Oil on canvas. 58.5 × 46.5 cm

11

Fiodor Rokotov. 1730s—1808
Portrait of E. Santi. 1785
Oil on canvas. 72.5 × 56 cm (oval)

12

Dmitry Levitsky. 1735—1822
Portrait of A. Kokorinov. 1769
Oil on canvas. 134 × 102 cm

13

Dmitry Levitsky. 1735—1822
Portrait of E. Nelidova. 1773
Oil on canvas. 164 × 106 cm

14

Dmitry Levitsky. 1735—1822
Portrait of P. Repnina. 1781
Oil on canvas. 62 × 50.5 cm

15

Anton Losenko. 1737—1773
The Sacrifice of Abraham. 1765
Oil on canvas. 202 × 157 cm

16

Fiodor Alexeyev. 1753/4—1824
View of the Palace Embankment from the Peter and Paul
Fortress in St. Petersburg. 1790s
Oil on canvas. 72 × 107 cm

17

Fiodor Alexeyev. 1753/4—1824
*View of the English Embankment
from Vasilyevsky Island in St. Petersburg*
Oil on canvas. 58 × 72.5 cm

18

Vladimir Borovikovsky. 1757—1825
Portrait of E. Arsenyeva. Second half of the 1790s
Oil on canvas. 71.5 × 56.5 cm

19

Vladimir Borovikovsky. 1757—1825
Portrait of F. Borovsky. 1799
Oil on canvas. 80.5 × 62.5 cm

20

Andrey Ivanov. 1776—1848
Kiev Youth's Act of Bravery during the Siege
of Kiev by the Pechenegs in 968 C. 1810
Oil on canvas. 204 × 177.5 cm

21

Orest Kiprensky. 1782—1836
Portrait of A. Schwalbe, the Artist's Father. 1804
Oil on panel. 78.2 × 64.1 cm

22

Orest Kiprensky. 1782—1836
Portrait of E. Avdulina. 1822
Oil on canvas. 81 × 64.5 cm

23

Orest Kiprensky. 1782—1836
Portrait of K. Albrecht. 1827
Oil on canvas. 196.5 × 138.5 cm

24

Vasily Tropinin. 1776—1857
The Guitar Player (Portrait of P. Vasilyev) 1830
Oil on canvas. 95 × 75 cm

25

Alexey Venetsianov. 1780—1847
Girl with a Birch-bark Jar. C. 1824
Oil on panel. 29.5 × 23.5 cm

26

Alexey Venetsianov. 1780—1847
Sleeping Shepherd Boy. Between 1823 and 1826
Oil on panel. 27.5 × 36.5 cm

27

Alexey Venetsianov. 1780—1847
Peasant Girl with Scythe and Rake (Pelagia).
Not later than 1825
Oil on panel. 22.5 × 17.5 cm

28

Grigory Soroka. 1823—1864
Fishermen. Scene at Spasskoye Country Estate
Second half of the 1840s
Oil on canvas. 67 × 102 cm

29

Nikifor Krylov. 1802—1831
Winter Landscape (Russian Winter). 1827
Oil on canvas. 54 × 63.5 cm

30

Alexander Alexeyev. 1811—1878
The Workshop of A. Venetsianov in St. Petersburg. 1827
Oil on canvas. 77 × 96 cm

31

Karl Briullov. 1799—1852
Italian Midday (An Italian Woman Gathering Grapes). **1827**
Oil on canvas. 64 × 55 cm

32

Karl Briullov. 1799—1852
The Last Day of Pompeii. 1833
Oil on canvas. 456.5 × 651 cm

33
Karl Briullov. 1799—1852
Portrait of the Sisters Shishmariov. 1839
Oil on canvas. 281×213 cm

34

Sylvester Shchedrin. 1791—1830
View of Sorrento, near Naples. 1820s
Oil on canvas. 95 × 137 cm

35
Fiodor Bruni. 1799—1875
The Bronze Serpent. 1841
Oil on canvas. 565 x 852 cm

36

Ivan Aivazovsky. 1817—1900
View of Odessa on a Moonlit Night. 1846
Oil on canvas. 122 × 190 cm

37

Alexander Ivanov. 1806—1858
Two Head-studies of a Slave
for the painting *Christ Appearing before the People.* 1833—57
Oil on paper. 51.5 × 70.5 cm

38

Alexander Ivanov. 1806—1858
Head of John the Baptist. Study for the painting
Christ Appearing before the People. 1833—57
Oil on paper. 64.2 × 58 cm

39

Alexander Ivanov. 1806—1858
Nude Boy. Study for the painting
Christ Appearing before the People. 1840—50s
Oil on canvas. 47.7 × 64.2 cm

40

Pavel Fedotov. 1815—1852
Portrait of N. Zhdanovich at the Piano. 1849
Oil on canvas. 24.5 × 19.2 cm

41

Pavel Fedotov. 1815—1852
The Major's Marriage Proposal. C. 1851
A version of the 1848 picture of the same name
Oil on canvas. 56 × 76 cm

42

Vasily Perov. 1834—1882
The Solitary Guitar Player. 1865
Oil on panel. 31.5 × 22 cm

43

Vasily Perov. 1834—1882
A Meal in the Monastery. 1865—76
Oil on canvas. 84 × 126 cm

44

Nikolay Yaroshenko. 1846—1898
The Old and the Young. 1881
Oil on canvas. 90 × 100 cm

45

Ivan Kramskoy. 1837—1887
Miná Moiseyev. Study for the painting
Peasant with a Bridle. 1882
Oil on canvas. 65 × 45 cm

46

Fiodor Vasilyev. 1850—1873
Scene on the Volga. Barques. 1870
Oil on canvas. 67 × 105 cm

47

Fiodor Vasilyev. 1850—1873
Bog in a Forest. Autumn. 1872—73
Oil on canvas. 81 × 111.5 cm

48

Nikolay Gay. 1831—1894
The Last Supper. 1863
Oil on canvas. 283 × 382 cm

49

Ivan Shishkin. 1832—1898
Oaks. 1887
Oil on canvas. 147 × 108 cm

50

Ivan Shishkin. 1832—1898
Leaves of Grass. Study. 1892
Oil on canvas. 24.7 × 39.6 cm

51

Ivan Shishkin. 1832—1898
Mast-tree Grove. 1898
Oil on canvas. 165 × 252 cm

52

Ilya Repin. 1844—1930
The Volga Boatmen. 1873
Oil on canvas. 131.5 × 281 cm

53

Ilya Repin. 1844—1930
Portrait of V. Stasov, Music and Art Critic. 1900
Oil on canvas. 106.5 × 71.5 cm

54

Ilya Repin. 1844—1930
*The Zaporozhye Cossacks Writing
a Mocking Letter to the Turkish Sultan.* 1880—91
Oil on canvas. 203 × 358 cm

55

Ilya Repin. 1844—1930
Portrait of K. Pobedonostsev. Study for the painting
Formal Session of the Council of State. 1903
Oil on canvas. 68.5 × 53 cm

56

Vasily Surikov. 1848—1916
The Taking of a Snow Fortress. 1891
Oil on canvas. 156 × 282 cm

57

Vasily Surikov. 1848—1916
Suvorov's Army Crossing the Alps in 1799. 1899
Oil on canvas. 495 × 373 cm

58

Arkhip Kuinji. 1841(?)—1910
Winter. Spots of Moonlight on the Snow. 1898—1908
Oil on paper mounted on canvas. 39 × 53.5 cm

59

Vasily Polenov. 1844—1927
Christ and the Woman Taken in Adultery. 1888
Oil on canvas. 325 × 611 cm

60

Vasily Polenov. 1844—1927
In the Park. The Village of Veules in Normandy. 1874
Oil on canvas. 61 × 46 cm

61

Isaak Levitan. 1860—1900
Golden Autumn. Village. 1889. Partially repainted in 1898
Oil on canvas. 43 × 59 cm

62

Isaak Levitan. 1860—1900
A Meadow on the Verge of the Forest. 1898
Pastel on paper. 63.5 × 49 cm

63

Isaak Levitan. 1860—1900
Lake. Russia. 1899—1900
Oil on canvas. 149 × 208 cm

64

Valentin Serov. 1865—1911
Woman in a Cart. 1896
Oil on canvas. 48 × 70 cm

65

Valentin Serov. 1865—1911
Peter II and Princess Elizabeth Riding to Hounds. 1900
Tempera and gouache on paper pasted on cardboard. 41 × 39 cm

66

Valentin Serov. 1865—1911
The Rape of Europa. Sketch. 1910
Tempera and gouache on cardboard. 40 × 52 cm

67

Valentin Serov. 1865—1911
Portrait of O. Orlova. 1911
Oil on canvas. 237.5 × 160 cm

68

Valentin Serov. 1865—1911
Bathing a Horse. 1905
Oil on canvas. 72 × 99 cm

69

Valentin Serov. 1865—1911
Portrait of Ida Rubinstein. 1910
Tempera and charcoal on canvas. 147 × 233 cm

70

Mikhail Vrubel. 1856—1910
The Bogatyr. Decorative panel. 1898
Oil on canvas. 321.5 × 222 cm

71
Mikhail Vrubel. 1856—1910
Six-winged Seraph. 1904
Oil on canvas. 131 × 155 cm

72

Mikhail Vrubel. 1856—1910
*Portrait of a Lady in a Violet Dress
(the Artist's Wife)*, unfinished
Oil on canvas. 160 × 130 cm

73

Abram Arkhipov. 1862—1930
A Festive Day in Spring (On a Visit). 1915
A version of the 1914 picture *Guests*
Oil on canvas. 105 × 154 cm

74

Abram Arkhipov. 1862—1930
Washerwomen. First variant
of a similarly entitled picture of 1901
Oil on canvas. 97 × 65.5 cm

75

Konstantin Savitsky. 1845—1905
Off to War. 1888
Oil on canvas. 207.5 × 303.5 cm

76

Mikhail Nesterov. 1862—1942
The Taking of the Veil. 1898
Oil on canvas. 178 × 195 cm

77
Mikhail Nesterov. 1862—1942
Portrait of the Artist's Daughter. 1906
Oil on canvas. 175 × 86.5 cm

78

Andrey Riabushkin. 1861—1904
A Seventeenth Century Merchant Family. 1896
Oil on canvas. 143 × 213 cm

79

Andrey Riabushkin. 1861—1904
*They are Coming! (Muscovites Watching the Entry of
a Foreign Embassy into Moscow
at the End of the Seventeenth Century).* 1901
Oil on canvas. 204 × 102 cm

80

Victor Borisov-Musatov. 1870—1905
Self-portrait with the Artist's Sister. 1898
Oil on canvas. 143 × 177 cm

81

Victor Borisov-Musatov. 1870—1905
Spring. 1901
Oil on canvas. 71 × 98 cm

82

Leon Bakst. 1866—1924
Portrait of S. Diaghilev with Nurse. 1906
Oil on canvas. 161 × 116 cm

83

Alexander Benois. 1870—1960
Venetian Garden. Versailles. 1910
Water-colour, gouache and white on cardboard. 48.4 × 63.7 cm

84

Konstantin Somov. 1869—1939
Portrait of the Artist A. Ostroumova. 1910
Oil on canvas. 87 × 63 cm

85

Konstantin Somov. 1869—1939
Winter. Skating-rink. 1915
Oil on canvas. 49 × 58 cm

86

Yevgeny Lanceray. 1875—1946
St. Petersburg at the Beginning of the 18th Century. 1906
Tempera on paper. 58.5 × 111.5 cm

87

Nikolay Roerich. 1874—1947
The Slavs on the Dnieper. 1905
Tempera on cardboard. 67 × 89 cm

88

Alexander Golovin. 1863—1930
A Street in Sevilla
Sketch of the decor for Bizet's opera *Carmen*. 1906
Tempera on paper pasted on cardboard. 69 × 101 cm

89

Alexander Golovin. 1863—1930
*Portrait of F. Shaliapin as Boris Godunov
in Mussorgsky's opera of the same name.* 1912
Tempera and foil on canvas. 211.5 × 139.5 cm

90

Konstantin Yuon. 1875—1958
Sunny Spring Day. The St. Sergius Posad. 1910
Oil on canvas. 87 × 131 cm

91

Philip Maliavin. 1869—1940
Two Peasant Girls. 1905
Oil on canvas. 205 × 159 cm

92

Igor Grabar. 1871—1960
Pears. Still Life. 1915
Oil on canvas. 73.5 × 60.5 cm

93

Vasily Rozhdestvensky. 1884—1963
Still Life with Coffee-pot and Cup. 1913
Oil on canvas. 82.5 × 71 cm

94

Konstantin Korovin. 1861—1939
Lilacs. Still Life. 1915
Oil on canvas. 97 × 73 cm

95

Konstantin Korovin. 1861—1939
Portrait of Fiodor Shaliapin. 1911
Oil on canvas. 65 × 81 cm

96

Zinaida Serebriakova. 1884—1967
Peasants. 1914
Oil on canvas. 123.5 × 98 cm

97

Alexander Kuprin. 1880—1960
Cactus and Fruits. Still Life. 1918
Oil on canvas. 97 × 113.5 cm

98

Boris Kustodiyev. 1878—1927
Shrovetide. 1916
Oil on canvas. 80 × 190.5 cm

99

Boris Kustodiyev. 1878—1927
A Merchant's Wife Drinking Tea. 1918
Oil on canvas. 120 × 120 cm

100

Ilya Mashkov. 1881—1944
Loaves. Still Life
Oil on canvas. 105 × 133 cm

101

Ilya Mashkov. 1881—1944
Still Life with Fan. 1922
Oil·on canvas. 145 × 127.5 cm

102

Nathan Altman. 1889—1970
Portrait of Anna Akhmatova. 1915
Oil on canvas. 123.5 × 103.2 cm

103

Pavel Kuznetsov. 1878—1968
Shearing Sheep
Tempera and pastel on canvas. 77.5 × 81.5 cm

104

Kuzma Petrov-Vodkin. 1878—1939
A Mother. 1915
Oil on canvas. 107 × 98.5 cm

105

Kuzma Petrov-Vodkin. 1878—1939
Herring. 1918
Oil on cloth. 58 × 88.5 cm

106

Kuzma Petrov-Vodkin. 1878—1939
Morning Still Life. 1918
Oil on canvas. 66 × 88 cm

107

Boris Kustodiyev. 1878—1927
*Festivities Marking the Opening of the Second Congress of
the Comintern and a Demonstration on Uritsky (Palace)
Square on July 19, 1920.* 1921
Oil on canvas. 133 × 268 cm

108

Alexander Osmiorkin. 1892—1953
The Taking of the Winter Palace. 1927
Oil on canvas. 300 × 173 cm

109

Yefim Cheptsov. 1874—1950
Marking Cooperative Day in a Village. 1926
Oil on canvas. 70 × 95 cm

110

Piotr Konchalovsky. 1876—1956
Still Life with Brocade and Coffee-pot. 1919
 Oil on canvas. 103.5 × 108 cm

111

Piotr Konchalovsky. 1876—1956
The Novgorodians. 1925
Oil on canvas. 138 × 181 cm

112

Rudolf Frenz. 1888—1956
Market at Ust-Sysolsk. 1922
Oil on canvas. 104 × 134 cm

113

Alexander Shevchenko. 1883—1948
Woman in Green. 1932
Oil on canvas. 118 × 96 cm

114
Alexander Deyneka. 1899—1969
Running. 1934
Oil on canvas. 235 × 260 cm

115

Semion Pavlov. 1893—1941
Winter. 1924
Oil on canvas. 110 × 125 cm

116

Konstantin Yuon. 1875—1958
Young People of the Moscow Suburbs. 1926
Oil on canvas. 59 × 67 cm

117

Alexander Samokhvalov. 1894—1971
Young Woman Worker. 1928
Oil on canvas. 65 × 50.5 cm

118

Mikhail Nesterov. 1862—1942
Portrait of the Surgeon S. Yudin. 1933
Oil on canvas. 99 × 80 cm

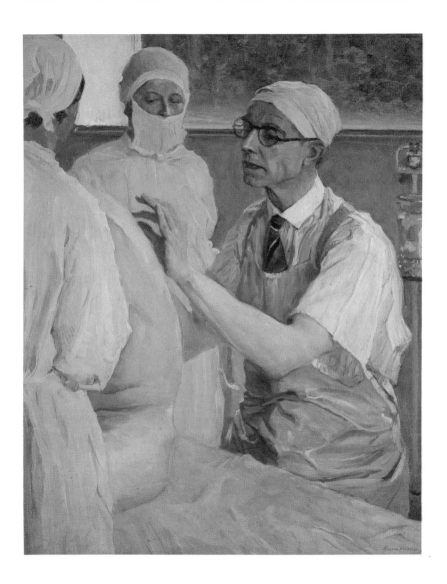

119

Alexander Shevchenko. 1883—1948
Still Life with Guitar. 1933
Oil on canvas. 50 × 77 cm

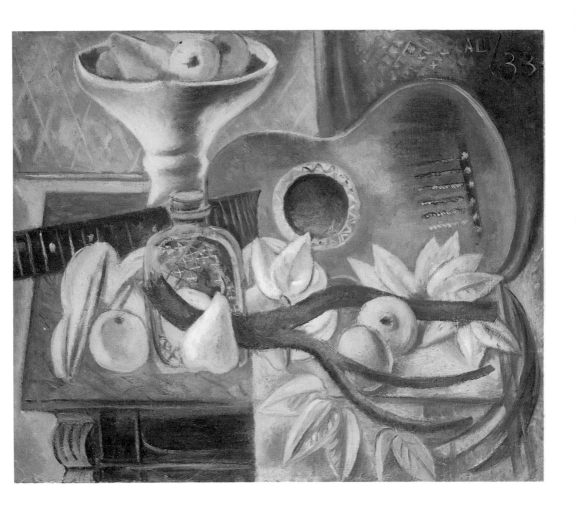

120

Sergey Gerasimov. 1885—1964
Bouquet of Water-lilies. Still Life. 1938
Oil on canvas. 100 × 71 cm

121

Sergey Gerasimov. 1885—1964
Oath of the Siberian Partisans. 1933
Oil on canvas. 173 × 257 cm

122

Arkady Rylov. 1870—1939
Autumn on the River Tosna. 1920
Oil on canvas. 78 × 101 cm

123

Arkady Rylov. 1870—1939
Forest River. 1929
Oil on canvas. 86 × 121.9 cm

124

Arkady Rylov. 1870—1939
Lenin in Razliv. 1934
Oil on canvas. 126.5 × 212 cm

125

Yuri Pimenov. Born 1903
Portrait of Varia Shitakova. 1935
Oil on canvas. 90.5 × 70.5 cm

126

Alexander Deyneka. 1899—1969
The Defence of Sevastopol. 1942
Oil on canvas. 200 × 400 cm

127

Arkady Plastov. 1893—1972
Vitia the Herdsboy. 1951
Oil on canvas. 121 × 186 cm

128

Arkady Plastov. 1893—1972
Summertime. 1953—54
Oil on canvas. 159 × 113 cm

129

Arkady Plastov. 1893—1972
Midday. 1961
Oil on canvas. 174 × 231 cm

130

Alexander Osmiorkin. 1892—1953
Leningrad. "New Holland". 1945
Oil on canvas. 100 × 75 cm

131

Pavel Korin. 1892—1967
Portrait of Renato Guttuso. 1961
Oil on canvas. 115 × 112 cm

132

Geliy Korzhev. Born 1925
Homer (Workers' Studio)
Left panel of the triptych *Communists*. 1958—60
Oil on canvas. 285 × 128 cm

133

Geliy Korzhev. Born 1925
Parting. 1967
Oil on canvas. 200 × 200 cm

134

Piotr Fomin. Born 1919
A Windy Day. 1965
Oil on canvas. 68 × 86 cm

135

Semion Chuikov. Born 1902
Song of a Coolie
Central panel of the triptych *Simple People of India.* 1959
Oil on canvas. 137 × 170 cm

136
Viacheslav Zagonek. Born 1919
After the Rainstorm. 1961
Oil on canvas. 170 × 267 cm

137

Olga Bogayevskaya. Born 1915
Birthday Party. 1960
Oil on canvas. 150 × 180 cm

138

Yevsey Moiseyenko. Born 1916
The Reds Have Come. 1961
Oil on canvas. 200 × 360 cm

139

Yevsey Moiseyenko. Born 1916
Comrades-in-arms. 1963—64
Oil on canvas. 195 × 130 cm

140

Victor Ivanov. Born 1924
Family. Year 1945. 1964
Oil on canvas. 175 × 257 cm

141

Vladimir Gavrilov. 1923—1970
The Joyous Month of March. 1960
Oil on canvas. 165 × 320 cm

142

Alexey Yeriomin. Born 1919
Mothers' Thoughts. 1969
Oil on canvas. 210 × 250 cm

143

Anatoly Levitin. Born 1922
On a Warm Day. 1957
Oil on canvas. 190 × 122 cm

144

Alexander Smolin. Born 1927
Piotr Smolin. Born 1930
Polar Explorers. 1961
Oil on canvas. 157 × 294 cm

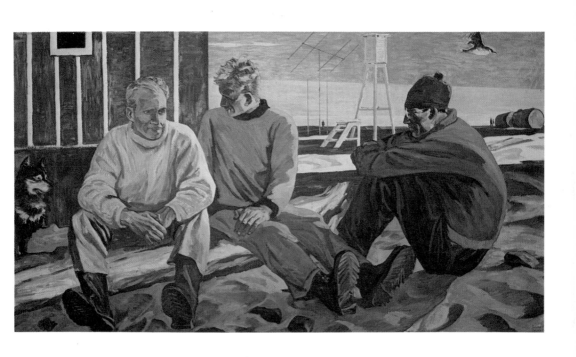

The Russian Museum. Painting

Aurora Art Publishers. Leningrad. 1974

Государственный Русский музей. Живопись

Автор вступительной статьи и составитель альбома Николай Николаевич Новоуспенский

Оформление художника Б. Н. Осенчакова. Перевод Л.М. Яковлевой. Редактор Г. В. Васильева. Редакторы английского текста Ю. И. Немецкий, Ю. С. Памфилов. Художественный редактор А. Р. Шилов. Технический редактор Н. А. Зубкова. Корректор И. Н. Стукалина. Подписано в печать 23/VIII 1974. Формат 72 х 72/16, бумага мелованная. Усл. печ. л. 18,48. Уч.-изд. л. 8,85. Изд. № 1403. Заказ 00102. (5-16). Издательство «Аврора». 191065, Ленинград, Невский пр., 7/9

Издано в СССР